EXPLORING DINOSAURS & PREHISTORIC CREATURES

PLESIOSAURS

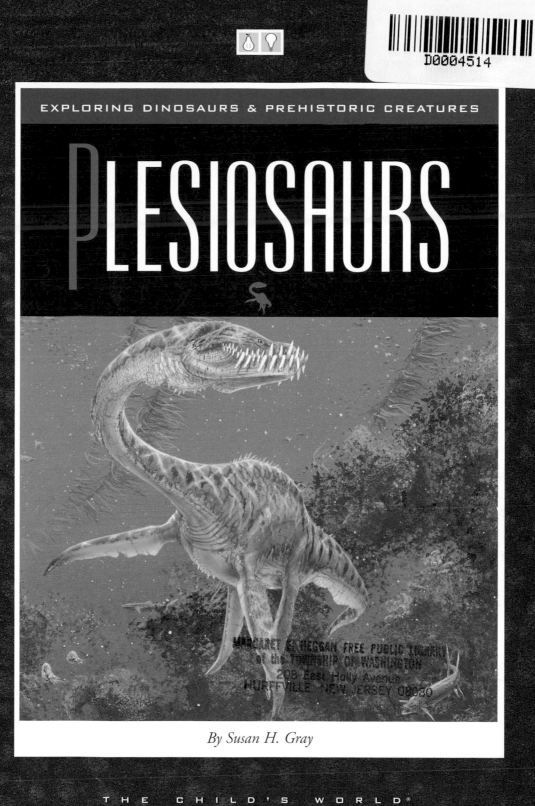

By Susan H. Gray

THE CHILD'S WORLD®
CHANHASSEN, MINNESOTA

The Child's World

Published in the United States of America by The Child's World®
PO Box 326, Chanhassen, MN 55317-0326
800-599-READ
www.childsworld.com

Content Adviser:
Brian Huber, PhD,
Curator, Department
of Paleobiology,
Smithsonian
National Museum
of Natural History,
Washington DC

Photo Credits: David Aubrey/Corbis: 7; Jason Hawkes/Corbis: 17;
Layne Kennedy/Corbis: 22; Mike Everhart, Oceans of Kansas Paleontology,
www.oceansofkansas.com: 4, 5; Mike Fredericks: 10; Muller/Gull/Taxi/Getty
Images: 9; Hulton|Archive/Getty Images: 18; the Granger Collection, New
York: 26; Douglas Henderson: 12; the Natural History Museum, London: 11, 13;
Chris Butler/Science Photo Library/Photo Researchers, Inc.: 6, 8, 15, 16; Fred
McConnaughey/Photo Researchers, Inc.: 19; Tom McHugh/Photo Researchers, Inc.:
20; Science Photo Library/Photo Researchers, Inc.: 25; South Australian Museum: 27;
Science VU/Visuals Unlimited: 23.

The Child's World®: Mary Berendes, Publishing Director

Editorial Directions, Inc.: E. Russell Primm, Editorial Director; Pam Rosenberg,
Line Editor; Katie Marsico, Associate Editor; Matthew Messbarger, Editorial Assistant;
Susan Hindman, Copy Editor; Melissa McDaniel, Proofreader; Tim Griffin/IndexServ,
Indexer; Olivia Nellums, Fact Checker; Dawn Friedman, Photo Researcher; Linda
S. Koutris, Photo Selector

Original cover art by Todd Marshall

The Design Lab: Kathleen Petelinsek, design; Kari Thornborough, page production

Library of Congress Cataloging-in-Publication Data
Gray, Susan Heinrichs.
  Plesiosaurs / by Susan H. Gray.
      p. cm. — (Exploring dinosaurs & prehistoric creatures)
  Includes index.
  ISBN 1-59296-367-6 (lib. bd. : alk. paper) 1. Plesiosauria—Juvenile literature.
I. Title.
  QE862.P4G73 2005
  567.9'37—dc22   2004018065

TABLE OF CONTENTS

CHAPTER ONE

ROCK SHOPPING

Styxosaurus (STIK-so-SAWR-uss) glided along in the shallow water. Every few seconds, she lifted her mighty front flippers and then drew them back down in a powerful motion. With each stroke, her massive body surged forward. *Styxosaurus* wasn't even fully grown, but she was already one of the biggest creatures in the sea.

A Stysosaurus skeleton clearly shows the animals long, graceful neck.

As she swam, she held her long, graceful neck straight out in front of her body. From time to time, she dipped her head down to nudge the rocks

Scientists determined that a Styxosaurus *once swallowed these rocks, which allowed the reptile to break down any food in its stomach. Some experts believe that this process may also have helped the creature to dive underwater.*

on the seafloor. She was looking for some that were just the right

shape and size. Finally, she found some rocks that were perfect. She

scooped up one with her mouth. Then she lifted her head and swal-

lowed. The rock moved slowly down her throat and into her stomach.

Then *Styxosaurus* scooped up a larger rock and swallowed it. Next she

went after a heap of pebbles.

Plesiosaurs were meat eaters that hunted in prehistoric oceans. Although meat eaters sometimes swallowed rocks in order to break down their food, this practice was more common among ancient plant eaters.

After swallowing them all, she turned and swam out into deeper water. Now *Styxosaurus* was looking for some *real* food—a fish or squid perhaps. The rocks were not her meal. Instead, they would help break down her food. Whatever the plesiosaur (PLEE-see-o-SAWR) caught would end up in her stomach. The rocks would tumble about as she moved, pounding her food into mush.

CHAPTER TWO

WHAT WERE PLESIOSAURS?

Plesiosaurs were swimming **reptiles** that lived in the ocean from about 220 million to 65 million years ago. The word *plesiosaur* is taken from Greek words meaning "near lizard," because the animal looked so much like a lizard, another kind of reptile.

Believe it or not, plesiosaurs are related to this modern-day chameleon! These modern lizards are famous for being able to change the color of their skin.

While dinosaurs walked on Earth, giant plesiosaurs swam through the oceans.

However, the plesiosaurs were not lizards. They were swimming reptiles that lived at the same time as the dinosaurs.

Plesiosaurs had sleek bodies that were wide in the middle. Embedded in their belly flesh were extra ribs called gastralia (gas-TRAY-lee-uh). They also had large collarbones and large hip bones. As the creatures swam through the water, their gastralia, collarbones, and hip bones acted as a strong supporting skeleton for their swimming muscles.

The plesiosaurs had short, thick tails and four fleshy paddles, or flippers. The front edge of each flipper was thick and rounded. The back edge was thin. This shape is much like that of a modern sea turtle's flipper or a penguin's wing. The hand bones inside the flippers had fingers with many bones and joints. These made the flippers strong and flexible.

Plesiosaur fins looked similar to those of modern sea turtles. Some scientists believe that plesiosaurs may also have been able to use their fins to travel short distances on land.

Plesiosaurs could swing their necks sideways to grab food.

There were two main groups of plesiosaurs: the plesiosauroids (PLEE-see-o-SAWR-oids) and the pliosaurs (PLY-o-sawrz). The plesiosauroids had long necks and small heads. Some of them had such incredible necks that one early scientist said they were like "snakes threaded through the bodies of turtles."

The pliosaurs were built differently. They had short, muscular necks and large heads with powerful jaws. Members of both groups survived until about 65 million years ago. This was about the same time the last of the dinosaurs died out.

CHAPTER THREE

HOW DID PLESIOSAURS GET AROUND?

Most of the time, plesiosaurs moved about by swimming. At one time, scientists believed they swam by using their flippers as oars. The creatures pushed their paddles backward, shoving their bodies forward. Then they drew their paddles forward again for the next shove.

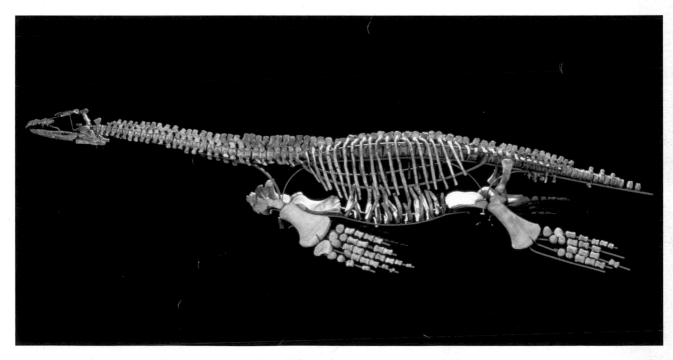

Scientists believe that different plesiosaurs swam at different speeds.

Now, scientists are rethinking this idea. They say that plesiosaurs more likely "flew" through the water just as sea turtles and penguins do. This means the plesiosaurs flapped their paddles up and down, rather than backward and forward.

Many scientists believe the plesiosaurs lived their whole lives in the water. Some believe the animals also came up on the land from time to time, probably to lay their eggs. Moving about on land would

Some prehistoric sharks existed at the same time as plesiosaurs.

If plesiosaurs ever came onto dry land, they probably moved like modern-day seals by using their flippers to travel short distances.

have been very awkward for these creatures. Their bellies would have dragged on the ground. Their big flippers would have been clumsy. Those with big bodies and long necks would not have moved very quickly. For these reasons, trips to the shore would have been quite dangerous. While on land, they could easily become **prey** for big meat-eating dinosaurs.

CHAPTER FOUR

MANY DIFFERENT PLESIOSAURS

Scientists have discovered many different kinds of plesiosaurs. *Elasmosaurus* (ee-LASS-mo-SAWR-us) was truly an incredible one. One of the longest plesiosaurs, *Elasmosaurus* grew up to 46 feet (14 meters) in length. More than half of that length was in its head and neck. Some skeletons have been found with more than 70 neck bones!

Cryptoclidus (KRIP-toe-KLY-duss) was another long-necked plesiosaur and grew to a length of 13 feet (4 m). It had about 100 sharp, curved teeth that interlocked when the animal's mouth closed. *Cryptoclidus* probably caught small fish, shrimp, and squid in this toothy trap.

The mighty *Kronosaurus* (KROE-no-SAWR-uss) was named after the **mythical** giant Kronos. *Kronosaurus* was a heavy, short-necked,

Elasmosaurus *lived between 80 million and 65 million years ago.*

big-headed animal that grew up to 30 feet (9 m) in length. Its head

was about one-fourth of its total body length.

Even bigger than *Kronosaurus* was *Liopleurodon* (LY-o-PLOOR-

uh-don). This giant of the sea grew to a length of 50 feet (15 m) and

had jaws more than 10 feet (3 m) long. With its short, thick neck and

Kronosaurus was a type of pliosaur.

heavy body, it almost looked like a whale. Its flippers were strong. It

took powerful swimming motions to move the huge creature through

the water.

Plesiosaurs were amazing reptiles. With their streamlined bodies

and winglike flippers, they were perfectly suited for life in the ocean.

GONE, BUT NOT FORGOTTEN

"There she is! There she is! I see her!" the man shouted. Everyone on the boat turned to look. Some raised binoculars to their eyes. Some squinted in the bright sunlight. No one said a word. They scanned the lake's surface in silence, hoping to see her. But no one saw anything except the choppy water. The man spoke again, this time quietly: "I know I saw her. I know I did." No one responded.

The people were on a boat, cruising a lake in Scotland called Loch Ness. For years, people in the area have claimed to see a lake creature they believe is a plesiosaur. Some say they have photographs of the animal. There are so many stories about the creature that people have even given it a name—Nessie.

Nessie isn't alone in the world. People in the United States have claimed to see

appear on T-shirts and postcards. They have their own Web sites and fan clubs. People hold parties in their honor and go out searching for them.

There's one problem, though. Nobody has ever found one. No plesiosaur has ever washed up on the shore. Not one has ever been caught in a fishing net. Scientists have scanned the lakes for these animals. Television crews have searched for them as well. Still nothing. But every year, more and more people say they've seen the creatures. This has been going on for years. Could plesiosaurs still be with us? What do you think of this mystery?

a similar monster in Lake Champlain. Over the last century, hundreds of people have said they saw "Champ" poking his head above the waves. People in Canada speak of Ogopogo, the creature living in one of their lakes. And a lake in Norway is said to be the home of giant, long-necked Thelma.

Some of these "sea monsters" have become quite popular. They

CHAPTER FIVE

WHAT DID PLESIOSAURS DO ALL DAY?

he daily life of a plesiosaur probably involved eating, swimming, and sleeping. The plesiosaurs ate all sorts of things. The small-headed ones fed on squid, shrimp, and small fish. The large-headed ones went after much bigger prey. They might have fed on sharks, large fish, and other plesiosaurs. With their muscular bodies and

Most people think of sharks as hunters instead of prey, but large-headed plesiosaurs considered prehistoric sharks a tasty meal.

Long-necked plesiosaurs such as Thalassomedon *(THAL-uh-SO-muh-don) came up for air but probably did not swim with their heads above the water like swans.*

short, thick necks, they were faster, more powerful swimmers than

their long-necked cousins.

As plesiosaurs swam about, they often had to swim near the

surface and lift their heads into the air. This gave them a chance to breathe in. They may have been able to hold their breath under the water for many minutes, just as modern-day seals do. Then they could have breathed out while still underwater.

At one time, many scientists believed that the long-necked plesiosaurs, such as *Elasmosaurus,* held their heads above water as they paddled along. This swanlike pose, they said, would allow the reptiles to scan the water for fish. Many people today think this was not the case. They point out that a long-necked plesiosaur could not stay balanced as it tried to lift its incredible neck straight up and keep swimming.

Besides swimming and eating, plesiosaurs also searched for rocks and tried to find mates. It is not certain whether plesiosaurs went up on the beach to lay eggs, or if they had live offspring. So no one knows how they treated their young.

A HEAVY STOMACH

Quite often, paleontologists (PAY-lee-un-TAWL-uh-jists) find small, unusual

rocks with plesiosaur skeletons. Paleontologists are scientists who study the remains of ancient living things. They look at fossil skeletons, footprints, and nests to figure out how things lived millions of years ago. Paleontologists have learned that these small rocks had something to do with the plesiosaurs' eating habits.

The rocks are called gastroliths (GASS-tro-liths). Plesiosaurs probably swallowed the rocks to help them digest food. Some modern-day birds do this. They swallow small bits of gravel, which remain inside the gizzard.

The gizzard is a tough, muscular part of the bird's stomach. As the gizzard muscles move, the gravel bumps around, helping to crush up food.

Gastroliths from plesiosaur stomachs are smooth, with rounded edges. Some are as small as marbles, while others are the size of baseballs. The biggest ones weigh more than 2 pounds (1 kilogram).

Over the years, paleontologists have suggested several other ideas as to why plesiosaurs swallowed rocks. Some said the animals sucked them up by accident as they fed along the seafloor. Others said they ate them on pur-

pose to get nutrients from them. Still others said that rocks in the belly would weigh down the plesiosaurs and keep them from bobbing to the surface. Whatever the reason, plesiosaurs sure swallowed those rocks. Skeletons have been found with more than 200 gastroliths in the stomach area!

CHAPTER SIX

THE HUNT FOR PLESIOSAURS

Some of the most interesting tales in paleontology involve plesiosaur discoveries. In England in the 1820s, Mary Anning became the first person to find a plesiosaur. At the time of the discovery, Mary was barely in her twenties, but she already had a sharp eye for spotting fossils. She also had a great hunger to learn more about them. Mary became one of the most famous fossil hunters in England. She provided fossils for schools and museums all over the country. One scientist even called her the Princess of Paleontology.

In the 1860s, another famous paleontologist got interested in plesiosaurs. Edward Drinker Cope was a scientist in the United States. He discovered *Elasmosaurus,* the plesiosaur with the incredibly long neck. He watched over the workers who dug up the skeleton, cleaned it, and pieced it together. When they were nearly finished, Cope carefully put the animal's skull in place. However, he made a huge mistake—one he regretted the rest of his life. Cope put the *Elasmosaurus* skull at the wrong end of the animal! He thought that the long string of bones could only be one thing—the reptile's whiplike tail.

He failed to see that *Elasmosaurus* had a short, thick tail. Soon afterward, Cope fixed his mistake. But some scientists never let him forget it.

In the 1980s, a beauti-

Mary Anning lived from 1799 to 1847.

Paleontologist Edward Drinker Cope is responsible for naming more than 1,000 fossilized animals.

ful *Leptocleidus* (LEP-toe-KLY-duss) skeleton was discovered in Australia. *Leptocleidus* was a plesiosaur that lived in shallow water. It grew to a length of 7 to 10 feet (2 to 3 m). *Leptocleidus* skeletons had been found before, but this one was special.

Over millions of years, the skeleton had turned to **opal.** Some opalized fish bones were even found in the creature's stomach area. In a very slow process, tiny particles of opal had replaced the tiny particles of bone in both the plesiosaur and its fish dinner.

People are making wonderful discoveries all the time. Plesiosaur bones and gastroliths show up in fields and on hillsides. They're discovered near cities and out in the country. Perhaps a plesiosaur is not far from your home, just waiting to be found.

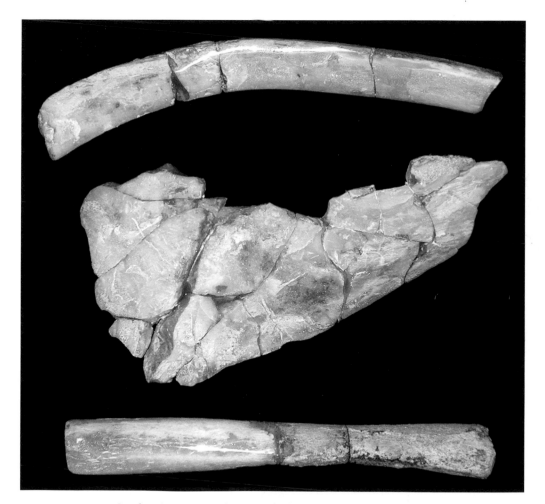

Opalized plesiosaur bones provide scientists with additional clues about the once-fierce reptile that ruled Earth's oceans.

Glossary

ancient (AYN-shunt) Something that is ancient is very old; from millions of years ago. Paleontologists study ancient life.

binoculars (buh-NOK-yuh-lurz) Binoculars are instruments used to see things far away. People use binoculars to see animals in the distance.

fossil (FOSS-uhl) A fossil is something left behind by an ancient plant or animal. Paleontologists look at fossil skeletons, footprints, and nests to figure out how things lived millions of years ago.

mythical (MITH-ih-kuhl) Something that is mythical is not real or true; it is based on a story. The mighty *Kronosaurus* was named after the mythical giant Kronos.

nutrients (NOO-tree-uhnts) Nutrients are things in food that are needed for good health. Some people said that plesiosaurs ate rocks on purpose to get nutrients from them.

opal (OH-puhl) An opal is a type of gem that is often milky white yet appears to give off many different colors depending on how the light strikes it. Over millions of years, one plesiosaur skeleton turned to opal.

prey (PRAY) Animals that are hunted and eaten by others are called prey. While on land, plesiosaurs could easily become prey for big meat-eating dinosaurs.

reptiles (REP-tilez) Reptiles are air-breathing animals that have a backbone and are usually covered with scales or plates. Plesiosaurs were swimming reptiles that lived at the same time as the dinosaurs.

Did You Know?

▶ Some of the first scientists to write about plesiosaurs really used their imaginations. One said they were "extinct monsters of the ancient Earth." Another said their necks were "like snakes, twisting and knotting themselves together."

▶ Plesiosaur remains have been found on every continent of the world—even Antarctica.

▶ Mary Anning started collecting fossils when she was a little girl. At one time, she even helped support her family by selling them.

▶ Scientists in Australia gave the name Eric to the opalized plesiosaur. They also gave the name Wanda to the fish found in its stomach!

How to Learn More

AT THE LIBRARY

Lambert, David, Darren Naish, and Liz Wyse. *Dinosaur Encyclopedia: From Dinosaurs to the Dawn of Man.* New York: Dorling Kindersley, 2001.

Palmer, Douglas, Barry Cox (editor). *The Simon & Schuster Encyclopedia of Dinosaurs & Prehistoric Creatures: A Visual Who's Who of Prehistoric Life.* New York: Simon & Schuster, 1999.

ON THE WEB

Visit our home page for lots of links about plesiosaurs:
http://www.childsworld.com/links.html
NOTE TO PARENTS, TEACHERS, AND LIBRARIANS: We routinely verify our Web links to make sure they're safe, active sites—so encourage your readers to check them out!

PLACES TO VISIT OR CONTACT

AMERICAN MUSEUM OF NATURAL HISTORY
*To view numerous fossils and learn
more about prehistoric creatures*
Central Park West at 79th Street
New York, NY 10024-5192
212/769-5100

CARNEGIE MUSEUM OF NATURAL HISTORY
To view a variety of dinosaur skeletons, as well as fossils of other extinct animals
4400 Forbes Avenue
Pittsburgh, PA 15213
412/622-3131

SMITHSONIAN NATIONAL MUSEUM OF NATURAL HISTORY
To see several fossil exhibits and take special behind-the-scenes tours
10th Street and Constitution Avenue NW
Washington, DC 20560-0166
202/357-2700

The Geologic Time Scale

CAMBRIAN PERIOD

Date: 540 million to 505 million years ago
Most major animal groups appeared by the end of this period. Trilobites were common and algae became more diversified.

ORDOVICIAN PERIOD

Date: 505 million to 440 million years ago
Marine life became more diversified. Crinoids and blastoids appeared, as did corals and primitive fish. The first land plants appeared. The climate changed greatly during this period—it began as warm and moist, but temperatures ultimately dropped. Huge glaciers formed, causing sea levels to fall.

SILURIAN PERIOD

Date: 440 million to 410 million years ago
Glaciers melted, sea levels rose, and Earth's climate became more stable. Plants with vascular systems developed. This means they had parts that helped them conduct food and water.

DEVONIAN PERIOD

Date: 410 million to 360 million years ago
Fish became more diverse, as did land plants. The first trees and forests appeared at this time, and the earliest seed-bearing plants began to grow. The first land-living vertebrates and insects appeared. Fossils also reveal evidence of the first ammonoids and amphibians. The climate was warm and mild.

CARBONIFEROUS PERIOD

Date: 360 million to 286 million years ago
The climate was warm and humid, but cooled toward the end of the period. Coal swamps dotted the landscape, as did a multitude of ferns. The earliest reptiles appeared on Earth. Pelycosaurs such as *Edaphosaurus* evolved toward the end of the Carboniferous period.

PERMIAN PERIOD

Date: 286 million to 248 million years ago
Algae, sponges, and corals were common on the ocean floor. Amphibians and reptiles were also prevalent at this time, as were seed-bearing plants and conifers. This period ended with the largest mass extinction on Earth. This may have been caused by volcanic activity or the formation of glaciers and the lowering of sea levels.

TRIASSIC PERIOD

Date: 248 million to 208 million years ago
The climate during this period was warm and dry. The first true mammals appeared, as did frogs, salamanders, and lizards. Evergreen trees made up much of the plant life. The first dinosaurs, including *Coelophysis*, existed on Earth. In the skies, pterosaurs became the earliest winged reptiles to take flight. In the seas, ichthyosaurs and plesiosaurs made their appearance.

JURASSIC PERIOD

Date: 208 million to 144 million years ago
The climate of the Jurassic period was warm and moist. The first birds appeared at this time, and plant life was more diverse and widespread. Although dinosaurs didn't even exist in the beginning of the Triassic period, they ruled Earth by Jurassic times. *Allosaurus, Apatosaurus, Archaeopteryx, Brachiosaurus, Compsognathus, Diplodocus, Ichthyosaurus, Plesiosaurus,* and *Stegosaurus* were just a few of the prehistoric creatures that lived during this period.

CRETACEOUS PERIOD

Date: 144 million to 65 million years ago
The climate of the Cretaceous period was fairly mild. Many modern plants developed, including those with flowers. With flowering plants came a greater diversity of insect life. Birds further developed into two types: flying and flightless. Prehistoric creatures such as *Ankylosaurus, Edmontosaurus, Iguanodon, Maiasaura, Oviraptor, Psittacosaurus, Spinosaurus, Triceratops, Troodon, Tyrannosaurus rex,* and *Velociraptor* all existed during this period. At the end of the Cretaceous period came a great mass extinction that wiped out the dinosaurs, along with many other groups of animals.

TERTIARY PERIOD

Date: 65 million to 1.8 million years ago
Mammals were extremely diversified at this time, and modern-day creatures such as horses, dogs, cats, bears, and whales developed.

QUATERNARY PERIOD

Date: 1.8 million years ago to today
Temperatures continued to drop during this period. Several periods of glacial development led to what is known as the Ice Age. Prehistoric creatures such as glyptodonts, mammoths, mastodons, *Megatherium,* and saber-toothed cats roamed Earth. A mass extinction of these animals occurred approximately 10,000 years ago. The first human beings evolved during the Quaternary period.

Index

About the Author

Susan H. Gray has bachelor's and master's degrees in zoology and has taught college-level courses in biology. She first fell in love with fossil hunting while studying paleontology in college. In her 25 years as an author, she has written many articles for scientists and researchers, and many science books for children. Susan enjoys gardening, traveling, and playing the piano. She and her husband, Michael, live in Cabot, Arkansas.